120

One Another

One Another

Dear Bill
I thought you deserved a decent
reading copy.

The Queen's Jubilee!

Peter Dale

W

THE WAYWISER PRESS

LONDON
2002

First published in 2002 by

THE WAYWISER PRESS

9 Woodstock Road, London N4 3ET, UK

T: +44 (0)20 8374 5526
F: +44 (0)20 8374 5736

waywiserpress@aol.com
www.waywiser-press.com

Editor
Philip Hoy

A CIP catalogue record for this book is available from the British Library

ISBN 1-904130-05-4

UK Distributor
Orca Book Services, 3 Fleets Lane, Poole, Dorset, BH15 3AJ, UK

N. American Distributor
Dufour Editions Inc., P.O. Box 7, Chester Springs, PA 19425, USA

Printed and Bound by
T.J. International Ltd., Padstow, Cornwall PL28 8RW, UK

Acknowledgements

This sequence is reprinted from *Edge to Edge: Selected Poems* by kind permission of Anvil Press Poetry Ltd.

Contents

The Lane

The willows hang their yellow swarms across
the turning by the hump-back bridge – that lane.
I still can make the river wash and swirl,
sucking the stonework underneath, and feel
pocking the wall-top the green grit of moss.
Like scratches down old movies, a thin rain.
No one turned there, not even boy and girl,
in all the years I passed. It's almost real.

I shan't walk now along that nameless lane.
(Only the memory pays for local maps.)
No face or place in the village to take me back.
Posit: the first aerial, then the stack,
a few houses expecting no one perhaps,
a child wondering away, nose to the pane.

Landscape

Me peeling away at a loose end of bark,
the silver birches; there, the stunted one,
a run of silver paint on rough grained wood,
and underfoot the usual dumping ground.
That childish hope when this was more a park
to peel some silver off and catch the sun
or make a mirror. Never any good.
But here's a trunk my hands can still surround.

Me peeling away at a loose end still,
watching the darkness grow beneath my hand,
scorched earth, scorched earth, and, staring in my face,
the old landscape I thought I left at will.
– Eyes, eyes that bear in mind this meagre land,
look back; hold me stronger than the place.

Dissolve

Face of a Greek tyro, and the neat hair
a cap of sparrows' wings, the lean thigh
in motion scooped and fluted, midriff bare –
I look for what it is that takes my eye,
and wish you deftest screw and steady aim
for no good reason but the longbow curve
your leg has, tensed; supply you with a name,
moth to a flame, that dark central reserve.
A sleepless night I had of it, your taut
body still poised to cue, your face, that face
pursuing, not pursued, in every thought.
And then a name clicked back into its place.
    Hard, to recall how long ago things last,
    my love, old love, my stand-in for the past.

Response

Dear, I should like you once in your life to be moved
by a printed phrase, not for the writer's sake,
still less for mine, but so that you could say
for once how odd it feels to learn your mood,
your feelings nursed along so nice and lush,
are nothing private to speak of, nor quite fresh,
my love, my dearest love. Though do not fret
yourself; there's something here to like or lump:

The dead tabby's paw clatter on the glass
when rain or shadow trick the eye, odd times,
can shake me more than what the mind replays
of one with her Shetland-pony fringe and glance,
or, worse, the moccasin-slouch, palm-forward style,
of that one from my student days, the plague.

Cone

Not dearest, but the nearest I have come
to love, such as it is, I'll watch you read,
your urchin hair within the lamp-light's cone,
the spray arrested on those curls that screen
your face. I always fell for that, but more
a street-light's cone, I don't know why, in rain,
an auburn head, the storm's panicky morse,
the lamp-light and a moment's ambered grace.

No, don't look up, my love, nor ask with eyes
what if we had our time again. Read on,
calves under thighs, your knees like new loaves,
and let me see you read my thoughts tonight:
the busby neatness of that auburn gone,
our destination dark and undisclosed.

Dialogue and Soliloquy

"Let's talk about the roses. They don't hurt,
do they? Red, spiky – red or maroon?
Soft, aren't they soft? And quite inert.
And look, there, look: the silly old moon
gormlessly dithering like a kid's balloon
left on a pond. That cloud making it spurt.
The darkness comes. Let's talk about it soon.
A snug fit, a shade closer than your skirt."

– I am the apple of his inner eye.
He wants to core me and he bores me, bores.
Once in a blue moon I'm two in his sky.
Cowish, I jump them for him on all fours.
I'm strip lighting and he wants it stark:
"Nearest, you come no closer than the dark."

A Little Light

Once it was a touch and then a tone of voice
and always promise of a turn of mind.
I could have touched your lashes any time
and you not bat an eyelid nor recoil.
Such calm. Your trust was always hard to take.
We've colonised a space now, an arm's reach,
filled with the things we touch on, books I need,
the plants you tend, green-fingered, self-contained.

Pressure, a touch, it never took much to work;
gentleness, warmth, the shadow mask on eyes
that give back nothing but a little light.
You turn from me, you grope for timeless words
and my dumb hands go out to you in time
to hold, like a flower's scent, your mind in mine.

The Rose

Such concentration on a single rose,
you look as though you watch it breathe the scent
till I am watching you and held intent,
your breath so hushed it hardly comes or goes.
What does it say to hold you in that pose,
that my lips cannot move, my hands invent?
Your words, they never tell me what is meant;
my hands can't touch the peace your body knows.

Pale bloom that gathers light from dusk, your hand
as white as whittled hazel without shine,
the sill and window where you hold quite still.
A word could break the spell ... I ache to stand
in for your eyes and grasp this rose in mine
as closely as your hand along the sill.

Insights

When shall we ever know each other more
than you this rose or me this quietude
of yours that breathes a presence through the room,
your slightest movement making stillness clear
as flickers of the firelight do. You pore
over the vase. You wouldn't know my mood,
nor I your insight to a rose's bloom;
your rose a focus, mine a misting sphere.

Move, love; finger the petal fallen there.
(Your palate's curvature, its touch to me.)
Now feel the micro-hesitance and know
the sense my hands have of your skin – your hair,
more like, that rounds their roughness in its flow.
So touch the rose, and in my hands you'll be.

Record

It is her microphone. She speaks with powers
I do not hear, no movement on her lips.
Dumb rose, record her thoughts, her fingertips
for after-comers. Make her the language of flowers.
– No, no, she listens. Others murmur here.
This is the poise that I have never caught.
To let go of a rose as of a thought,
the bloom untremored as her hand lifts clear.

Are roses still becalmed where Helen is?
The trees drop shadows; light ripples the leaves.
That time, held frame, of shadeless memories;
the light like glass. Oh, love, you turn again.
If only we let go as your hand reprieves
a rose, unmarked, and the daylight could be plain.

Talisman

Bellflowers, seldom seen now, stellar, trim,
on porcelain where the day is warm and clear
as flame within a candle's melting rim;
that squirl so delicately fellowed here.
– The trinket-well I gave you long ago
to cast a wistful spell that was your own.
And it became you, love. But now it's broken,
my clumsy hands: the light flawed with a mote.

It hurts, as if a talisman, now drained,
withdrew its gentle aura from you, though
you're just the same and do not seem aware.
But here's the perfect match at last obtained.
Throw out the first and who would ever know?
Yet no two days of summer make a pair.

Match

Someone who loved the clay and loved the flowers
made this and caught the look of day in it.
Not one who tried to see how exquisite
it was in loving me and my sad hours.
The broken one I'll save as rightly ours
and you will sometimes see me watch that split
and blur it out with wondering how we knit
our days together with such clumsy powers.

Someone who loved me gave this broken thing
and I will match it with the perfect one.
These two shall be for us a perfect match:
one past and one to come, as time may bring.
And since we don't know which of them is done
we may move gently and perfection snatch.

Silence

Cloud stilted along on two great spokes of light.
And then to enter the room, its shadow cool.
A bowl of roses, the oak-table, white blooms
like slow swans reflected in its pool, plumes
brushed by a moment's breeze. A dusty gold
fizzing a shaft of sun, the mullion's shade
leading across the carpet – shoulders bare,
shadowed by a great silence of cascading hair,

the woman sitting, focused within her mind,
(myself unseen) hands folded in her lap
cupping the darkness loosely like a bird,
book on the floor accordioned.
                                        To find you there,
presence to presence. Cloud happens to change
the light. You turn as though you heard it move.

Declination

That momentary declination of your head,
the water-chevron hairs along your nape,
revive an old attraction. I slowly drape
your shoulders, hold you there. You turn instead
your baffled squirrel look – and nothing said,
all lost. My love, some day I'll buy a cape
and every time your hair's in its great shape
I'll help you on with it to bow that head.

What binds us, dearest, is this touching grace.
It's like a cat's or in a squirrel's leap.
Or else, for me, the glossing of a beech.
But you know the dodge, the time and place.
I have to eavesdrop on your style of sleep –
your eyelids close and you are out of reach.

Aubade

Our hands have had their say time and again:
your quiet touch, the cat in the dog's shade,
a sneaking stroke of love in the shopping parade,
some grasp of shared experience in pain.

Dark in my long watch of your summer sleep,
I wonder what my hands would have to say
the day you die. And all the words that weigh
into the head make my flesh and blood creep

to you to wrest you closer from the night.
– Sleep on, my love, sleep in your cool bed.
May these cold hands never enter your head.
And in the morning may the breaking light
suffuse your lids with rose before you wake.
The first shadow on you my touch will make.

Shadow

Shadow of a leaf on a butterfly's wing,
solid as a beetle's wing-case, fine veneer.
I wait to hear it click down like a spring

the instant that the tortoise-shell flits clear.
I'm learning to be patient, love. You freeze.
My hold is less than light on you, that sheer

absorption, as you tense for flight or breeze.
Glacially, you edge forward now. I know
enough of you to see you mean to ease

your shadow over the wing and hold it so.
That daft stray lock of yours will almost reach.
You cannot make it stay. It's touch and go.

The shadow leaf snaps down in me like a screech.
I catch you off balance and without speech.

View

So much, so much ... I only have to reach
my hand to you, my fingers swaying the fine
hair of your nape as the breeze that field of wheat.
You hardly notice, though there comes to mind
a gentle lulling. And this pressure to hold
your mind to instances of mine – it seems
almost enough. These hands can trail a shoal
of lights along your hair and you will sleep.

And I would hold the gift of sleep for you.
No other gift so good, unless some tact
were in my hands to press on you the mood
of this great purple thunder-bank, flint-knapped
along the brink with light, or to attune
my sense of music to your stone-calm hands.

Music

Full of mortal longing the cor-anglais yearns.
I thought of Chatterton, the marvellous boy,
at least that painting in the Tate, the light
there, or that *April Love*, the rich mauves,
the light there much the same, as she half turns
and looks inward. Her song would surely cloy.

    An English wood and autumn burning late,
    the boat-knock branches as the light breeze moves,
    those kipper-coloured leaves and, feather-frail,
    one poplar. The pile of this moss so smooth,
    so cool to stroke. A squirrel, brown, ears frayed,
    quizzical; sun enough to make it muse.

His reaper sang contralto in this cadence.
Will no one tell me what she hears, my music?

Her Concentration on a Nutshell

They used to make us cockleshells for the bath.
You open them so gently, knife down the seam.
Uncrinkle the kernel, though. What worlds of earth
would round out from the walnut; not the same,
oh, not the same as ours! Another scale.
The mind it is, inside the head. (He'd like
to crack my codes, edge deep into the skull.)
I part the hemispheres with a nuclear click.

Colour of blanched almond, these firm thighs,
and curved the same where they surface in the bath.
This English pallor, smooth and hazed. – All space
is curved and he has reached his bound in these.
He wants me all and he can have them both.
Come, tan of walnut juice, you add some spice!

Pressed

These flowers are a gentleness in my grasp.
My hands harbour the haft-hold too long,
their lightest drift to you a weathered rasp.
These slight flowers give as the wind grows strong.

This wide reach of evening, all that surf
of cloud-rack, the thunder-bank's great rift,
the rayless sun no more than a clean pine kerf.
Flowers and hand one shadow on the drift.

See, we could press them there against your skin
and mine, mementos of our day – though much
the better in a book. Words always win.
We'd have to stay like this all night in touch.

Love, in your most private grief, my hands
have never touched you without desire to have.

Sunset and Storm

Cool grass-blades creep up and over my hand.
The old blaze of sunset deepens the thunder-bank
on green-tops wet with light, liftless, tranquil.
All's said and done, my love. You understand,
the years I have assumed, this peace before storm.
(Eye blinked by the wingless flight-phase of a bird.)
This wait that never varies for leaves stirred
by the first gust, the first rain, chill, enormous.

Too long I've let these things speak for me.
I can survive only as long as your mind.
Hold instances of mine. This bracelet of bone
that splays your hand in the drenched grass. You're free.
Go in. Wash off the mud. But leave behind
the link of skin that binds you in your own.

Deed of Gift

It's not enough. Not personal enough.
Landlubbers all have fallen for this time.
Something that pulls the mind up sharp like a lime,
I need, none of this sentimental stuff.

I'll give you a pendant watch. It's not much
but wear it always under your blouse to tell
a moment you can only show yourself.
It will take your breath away, cold to the touch.

I'll clip the catch for you. Nod down your neck,
hold still. But my hands, love, are cold, so cold.
There now. Your pulse is beating the time told.
I promise you'll only hear the odd second

like a skipped beat: my hands chill on your nape
and your thin skin cringing up like crape.

Shades

My hand's reach larger than life upon the blind,
the light so limited that the dark leaks in.
You shudder at the shape in mind, you say;
a branch wuthered against the window, bare,
hag-black to stifle you – until my hand,
soft as a shadow, brushes away your cry.
Dark promises, my love, lie candid there.
I've just the ghost of a touch to sidle down
your spine. Once a shadow, always a ghost.
Remember among windswept oaks or cloistral beech
these hands. They'll haunt your body mostly there.
How they'll remember at arm's reach you comb
        and slowly comb your hair until it gleams
        satisfactorily with my sweat. Sweet dreams.

Moon

These hands are so old. I don't know what to think.
They hold their own when I have lost my grip.
They know of ways around that you let slip.
You tremor like water just above the brink.

I watch your face for thoughts, for mood – your face
wizened a moment by movements soft as time.
Look, love, I'll gather what your features mime.
Your eyes reflect a light I cannot place.

Now you are young again. In the low light
your skin-tone has the mother-of-pearl that blurs
the rimless moon in mist. That's the rare sight
you always bring to mind now, though you smile:
and what if that means frost and heavy furs?
You'd lie there still, my love, in all your style.

Frost

White crystals clear, lean over, melt away
as breath peels back along the frosted fence.
Moss-feints return. The wonder is all day
whether the grain, the green, will be as dense
when dusk returns, or white again with frost,
clinging like iron-filings, to the wood.
Again he breathes his warmth, all focus lost,
until the knot nets outwards as it should.

– So much you bring back as you bend, your hair
brushing the frost, and breathe to melt the white
upon a spider's web, taking good care
to break no thread. More frost, my love, tonight.

Like kids, my lips will melt a frost tonight,
a frost and frost of light along your lids.

Hand and Head

I sweat it out, your perfume in the heat;
the closest we have come, and dear enough
without this hankering for the deeper stuff.

And yet to know you like an open book,
my lost language never glossed completely.
You turn over again to a clean sheet.

Just once, perhaps, to read of my approach
under the cover of your sharpest look-out
calmly anticipated nook by nook.

In these arms also your need of surprise,
a stroke of genius rather than encroachment,
the craft say, of this fronded silver brooch.

"King Alfred ordered me made." How neat it lies,
a starry blur above foreshortened thighs.

The Shadow

She promised all. You gave me what you had:
your stillness centripetal to a room,
your gawky poise coaxing a rose to bloom,
barefoot, your heel-down, ballerina pad.

And yet you can't compete within her shadow.
In dreams, in anger, she surfaces, assuming
a sleeking otter-back of naked grooming
under the nylon, its flowing off so gradual.

Breast turning a propeller of light, she straddles
her stole, manoeuvring for the slowest zoom-in.
That once you stalked off in the pine-dark gloom
and she turned up in only your old plaid.

Bare, with your heel-down, ballerina pad,
your bird-launching laugh, how she skedaddled!

A Long Shot

Mad hikes over bracken, nettlebeds, wildflowers
to find a place no foot had trodden first.
I swore I'd remember every single hitch
but in the end you were too many for me.
You always were impossible. A place all ours,
there must be one, you say.
                            A struck tree,
the boggiest corner, midges at their worst,
its riven trunk straddled across the ditch.

Just as it fell, you say, the storm last night.
You have to walk on it in your high heels.
Your flaired skirt of blinding saffron peals
this way and that, my silent bell. One stone,
then you strap-hang on a willow, a real sight.
Hold it.
              And here you stand on tips of bone.

The Thunder Stone

Ten years and no memories to call our own,
you say, eyes scavenging across the field,
raking the sky-line for something it might yield.
(Basket creak of leaves by the dry-stone.)
Let's find a gap that no one else has known
and get an angle frost or wind revealed,
then with a seeded handful of earth concealed
or cones, my sparrows drying off, windblown.

– No, here's a chalky flint I split on flint;
our landscape on its surface and, inside,
these mirror-image, thunder-purpled skies.
All glint, and water will restore the glint.
They'll never fade to blue. This one we'll hide,
the other take – a match that never lies.

Storm

Your fear of lightning, my need of the storm.
The great pylons a pale shadow of the cloud
bouldered above us and your slight figure cowed.
Sky cracks like ice and the rain slow and warm.
Your hand in mine. I cannot hold your fear
and you can't draw the need from me, your head
so close I muffle up your other ear.
The two of us, you say, the two of us dead.

The power to drive a city in that flash,
all spent to burn a vacuum in the sky.
I watch it branch and you tense for the crash.
Big drops darken and connect across your dress.
Love, where we hold close we are bone-dry;
you cling, and what comes through is powerless.

Walk

I know, I know. It is only a dream,
but there are dogleg rivers I cannot cross
and paths in company I walk alone:
a certain tilt of willow, a touch of moss.
Yet still there come these moments when you seem
some distance with me in the placeless zone –
unless I catch sight of the knurled bough
angling the path I cannot quite say how.

Though, love, you must have paths and paths to walk.
How you might need my hand to bring you through.
(That flint split to a sky of thunder grey.)
And you might reach for me as now you do
and say: "That's betony, that broken stalk,
and that chink-chink's a thrush. They fix the day."

Bird's-Eye

We take an hour off in the watery sun.
Bird's-eye, you suddenly exclaim: minute,
a tiny pansy-type of a bleak blue.
I actually like the thing, the way it shuns
the eye, less brash than pansies.
                                Not the name,
you say, my mother called it that. You find
the name. It must be in the books.
                                I'll try,
love, though we know it's just to pass the day.

I'll find its name, and it will be the name
of that nothing we did to say we lived.
But bird's-eye, let the children say
until, when grown, they find its grassy dip
and wonder over what its true name is.
Birsy, love, the flower I cannot change.

Memento

A leaf. He's given me an autumn leaf,
faded, but never to perish with the fall.
The marvels of technology! Every least
serration, every vein and slightest fault
precisely sealed in burnished copper foil,
and yet so light. He'd even make a style
of dead leaves. I'll wear it over the void
of my breast. There, leaf to the closest eye.

Funny this catch ... And there's a pinpoint leak
the foil has left. The air will seep inside.
Brave new technique, and he has not the skill
this time to mend it. Slowly, slowly, leaf,
you'll sidle out on me, his secret sign,
built-in obsolescence of life under a skin.

One Another

I am that silent pool. I mirror, opaque.
I float the water-lilies, candescent flame,
and I reflect the imperturbable swan.
No cloud-race scuffs my surface; that stake
lays claim to my depths, leaving no wake.
Minnows dart bright silence, the perch aim.
Stones make rings around me and are gone.
I still the rain's trickle. I become a lake.

Her body flows from me in the night.
Like evening mist on a river, she comprehends
the darkness. As blossoms in the mist, the white
to white, my touch floats down to her and ends
somewhere unseen, drifting with the stream.
The fearful silence where dark waters gleam.

Dream

Your presence like a drug that does no harm
cannot enclose me from the trackless night.
Let me sleep now ... and your pervasive calm.
– Awareness hurtling down a rail of light,
it plummets headlong in the roaring ditch
where bones, a mildew green, clutch out their roots,
and blood seeps from a wound this stolid pitch
of ants that waver to yowls of distant brutes.

Let us rest now, love. The terror will keep.
Only in nightmare is it safe to scream.
All quietudes I have you manage to find;
I will not promise you my share of sleep.
Still waters widen the quiet in your dream.
Let us sleep now; the dark is to my mind.

Compact

For term of life you are determined mine.
Some tree is bound to shadow forth my reach:
no man whose hand has not the same design;
a touch or two of mine you'll have to teach.

And when you seek the years in the window pane,
a dog's claw scuffed along the street will pass
shiver on shiver down your spine again
like these nails scratching down your looking-glass.

And what would you ever do to change the line
your first sleep makes of eyelid into cheek
that you have never seen and I call mine?
This curl behind the ear that spoils your chic?

We are determined, love, for term of life,
and if we fold, it's blade into the knife.

Comfort

The slipping shoulder-strap – yet now with calm
I watch, and, yes, the old impatience still:
your thumb slips in, a neat barge of the arm
and comfort comes again; the slight cups fill
as hands pray backwards in a kid's quick drill:
naked you shiver in your ever green charm.
Such ingrained love of comfort in night's chill!
And then you leap in the dark without a qualm.

My comfort, you, whose comfort used to goad.
How do we do it? Arms in such a twist
all night. They'd cramp in moments if awake.
Sleepy, hoick my arm up over your waist.
Oh love, may such a comfort still hold good
the night your ghosts or mine begin to walk.

Present

This tiny squirrel ornament you chose
   to give me, knowing I love the miniature.
   You mean it for the smoky, bounding creature,
give me grace and lissomness, the fellow's
quizzical look. And, by some lucky chance,
   you have: they've slipped and made one darker pupil
   stare from the head, half-turned, as if the ill-
painted cone had caused him some perturbance.

You want to give all this. And I accept it.
   Cheeky fellow. Look, you couldn't guess
which hand he's in, so sleek and exquisite!
   Yet, love, it's only touches give such softness,
grace ... though hands, my hands that drowse your passive
shoulders feel more gentleness than they give.

Inklings

I came once on a place where a presence dwelt
that was no vestige of a living thing,
dank and foreboding, like a worldless suffering
condemned to leech into all life it felt;
the sudden brinking of a forest in the dark,
sheer on to silent waters, still as tar.
And now that place moves with me like a scar.

You plant your acorns, say we'll leave a mark.
– Love, let it be. The slant light clings to your hair.
The shadow of a flame, you block the sun.
What inkling of us would you nurture there
to brood upon the waters without form and void?
You loop a twig and lift a sunset spun
into the trees. You blow. All ghosts destroyed.

Fledgling

That fledgling falls up fluttering to a bough.
I see an autumn leaf reverse, you say;
and spurt ahead – a child making a play
to catch it up, the street forgotten now.

– Oh, love, suppose the mind holds more than sense,
and things we love may bear some lasting trait
of us that later minds may mediate,
something survive where mind once grew intense.

You would return where roses are in bloom,
a concentration round a rose's scent;
or in the spring with swifts to skim and zoom,
and I shall not be there to watch you ache
to enter flower or flight. Now, as you went,
you turn and breast the leaf-light, flake on flake.

Glimpses

Caught in the angle of the steps a shoe brad,
a crushed packet glinted; an ancient pool
of stagnant light wrinkled a tarmac roof.
An odd corner of the casual eye that had
Waterloo Bridge in mind, the pine-shaped, cool
scribbles of light. For days, like a reproof
too trivial to tell, that litter fixed my thought
with every glimpse of mine you'd never caught.

And one seen from a train: a Surrey field,
a crack willow with fishing withes that leant
across a nettled ditch where pollen lay
denting the surface tension. So long concealed
and nothing much to tell: a moment spent
without you, love; the moments build away.

Her Prophecy

Three days after my death I shall return.
I will return and find you not in grief
but lost in quietude now past belief,
gazing upon the frost of patterned fern
across the panes ghosted with mist and trees.
You shall be calm as my oaks ridged with rime,
for all that you could not possess in time
has vanished – haven't I? – with ease.

For now you know there's nothing in the oaks,
nothing of me; there never was. I meant
those steady hands to cup a whorling bud
like life so tight they crushed it into scent.
Your world, that could not be to flesh and blood,
has vanished. Peace be with you – till it chokes.

Hearing the Flowers

There you go. Catch the minutest shudder
of petals in the fire's draught, and there you are,
your book a bird ruffling feathers in air
chilled by the sudden rustle of a shadow.

It frightens me, the mind, where it will shelter.
Sit beside me. Keats, in this fragment here,
more warm and capable to me, toward her,
than in his chosen works. Lean on my shoulder.

We're into words again. You're in my hands.
I'll hold the book for you. Murmur aloud
the living lines the dying hand still haunts;
your head weighs on my heart its mortal load.
You lose the place in shaking out your hair.
My love, it's far too close for flowers in here.

Duotone

Hands, hands to touch me like a sparrow's wings
gliding across a puddle's little sky.

> Gentleness, pressure, closer than murmurings,
> the flesh-tones pearling where my fingers lie.

Suavity, suavity of fingers, skim and plane;
husks of his touch I liquefy – I'm air.

> A shadow blown across a field of grain,
> the drifting of my hands along her hair.

In dream his touch is softer than the dark;
all moods, all modes of thought at the fingertips.

> What keeps such softness from my least remark,
> gentleness, pressure, speechless on my lips?

> Darkness we thought to enter with a torch.

Blind in the night we're dumb from talking touch.

Spectrum

My darling has the rain at her fingertips,
sun in her hair. Steady, she aims to make
a local little rainbow. Time, do not shake
though silver crescents swirl around eclipse,
as watching with wonderful patience here I stand,
considering where on earth the light will break,
coloured with some conviction for her sake.
Soon she will have me drinking from her hand.

You kneel and pick up grains of dust in the swirl
of several drops to make your spectral band.
Love, turn. I catch the spectrum in your hair,
and you, you easily could raise your hand,
arrange those drops of light on the odd curl
and take my word for rainbows in the air.

Clear Stream

The water runs through my fingers, always will.
Remember when I tried to drink from yours?
But you're away again, and the earth scores
your shadow on the run. I watch it spill,
the stain of water dark and shapeless. Hair
that flows like water as you chase or shake
it willowing down. Most taken with the air,
then most you're mine, though hardly for my sake.

Sooner or later you'll come back to cool.
The ground's too wet for anything so bare.
You'll find a way, a cat and water-shy.
How long we'll wait for shade to seep and pool.
Flow like water, my eyes caught in your hair,
our time turning.

Moth-Light

The sun-blaze sinks again and the brittle sky
shells over, yellow, luminescent green.
The light rusts through the black foil of trees,
and a martin zigzagzigs in a last flight.
Shadows, shadows, mindless shadows rise.
The countless times we've lazed till the last gleam
crumbles from the clouds, and it seems peace
we never came to come to us in time.

Your body says it is. Long shadows seep
to you and tide into small pools of shade.
I watch. I watch you watch. So many repeats
and nothing to speak of. The light that studs your eye
is light that glitters in a drop of rain.
Light of my eye, you moth-light to the mind.

Dusk

The years in the window pane, the daffodils
leaning stiffly like children's paper windmills
    still toward evening, the mitre buds of lilac.
    Wood-scent your hair was; young, your face looks back.

You start, shivering, at a boy's cry like God
along the street, and watch a girl go slipshod
    in her mother's high heels. Earliest starlight
    and you'd make out new patterns in the night.

And my hand, still dark to white on yours, though wizened.
    Enough now, was it ever enough to hold you,
this touch no words came close to in the end?

Love, leave the crazy tock of moth to window,
    the lamp-light's cone an auburn head shines through.
Catch again the splendour of light in the wine-glow.

The Game

Now don't you fret. There is no other way.
Some time or other there must come an end.
What would you have? And how would it hurt less?
Come on, give me your hand, finish the game.
You'll see how softly I return its morse.
Then I shall get that good night's sleep
we never had those crazy times your sleek
shadow pranced and frescoed all four walls.

As I came out of darkness and found light,
and found it finer in your lively eye,
so into nothing I shall go and find
the cool moss of darkness was no lie.
I know where to turn. A starlit night;
take one of your walks now. I shan't mind.

Autumnal

Too close we breathe each other's tepid breath.
– The first time it was and meant to stick.
Late afternoon. A shoal of leaves windswept
across the window. You with your lousy gift
for drama: "The leaves are falling, I must fly."
Yet stayed to fling the window wide and catch
a leaf or two, then turned with a wet shine,
hair all over the place, one lacquered lash.

Autumn's hamming it up as ever again.
Odd angles like veins, the runnels down the pane.
A leaf with the rain's adhesion clings to the sill
against all gusts. My love, only last year
I willed that leaf to hold. The window chill
against my face, and your name coming clear.

The Oak

More shadow leaves than real on your old oak.
My touch more shadow than the day can clear.
Your face, a shade closer than the lure
of all the living; your body is the dark
beneath my hands. Was there ever light
enough for you? Was light ever enough?
Winter gave most. Now, love, you are the north
my memory steers from, late, so very late.

I cannot uproot an oak. I cannot move
the place I live, the mind derange its fix.
A few dead leaves lift on the aftermath.
We followed the foxgloves where the path forks;
it seems a way we never chose but took.
Now, love, I'm going down the other track.

Before Sleep

Barbaric ... yet I should have seen you dead,
and quelled the endless images of death
that rise up mouthing speechless from the depth
of time – your hand reaching again, condemned
to splay against a surface-tension stretched
like polythene. Your fingers whiten, press,
like children's noses, for rescue or to fend
me off. Oh make it clear. – There, on the breast,

a vein straggles like a silver birch.
Tell me it's not an image you intend.
Far love, I look with pity for the first
time ever on your body, feel a sense
of treason. It's finished, love. Leave off the frenzy.
We cannot even now be just good friends.

Revenant

My arm around you comforts me at night
that when the ghosts come you will not see,
nor the hooded santa in the gown all white
and trimmed with blood. You would wake free

to clear my eyes, your body calm with sleep;
you, warmest, who were never much of a dream,
my arm around you.
                    – Or nights you creep back round
to me, your hazy gown our scheming wraith.

My arm dragged in the dark across shroud white.
My blind-spot in our room. Oh love, what's wrong?
You left my bed so many nights, one night.
Be reasonable, love; no, not the white lace.
Wear the quilted black. And don't be long;
my arm lays only a little warmth in your place.

Clearing

After so long to fetch up with silver birch,
bracken inflating with the breeze, the dry
springy mat of needles, the mind's purchase,
where only homely ghosts retrace the by-ways.

That trunk, with all the torsion of a girl
elbowing her slip above her head, dead wish
or memory. (A life-long stepper-out, you were,
foot over silken splash with a cat's precision.)

No walks by still waters, hoping for seas,
nor where oaks writhe. These silver birch
will do; they always have, beyond all reason.
I shall not wander into you round here.
Winter is mine, the bare boughs emerging.
My ways have narrowed, these dry sticks my clearing.

Moth

A flake of wood, chip off the old block,
that's what you must be. And as for me,
I must be cracking up. Why otherwise
this inordinate affection for a moth,
the size of a fingernail? And on my clean
grey shirt. D'you think it's elm or pine?
D'you too seek refuge from the local woods?
The rust corrupts here. Tell me, what's the pull?

Flit. To the skirting-board. Why home on me?
Find yourself some bare and natural wood.
I won't clean too hard. I don't want to kill you.
Stay solo. More of you will pull the wool
over my eyes that way. No, out of that beam!
– Did she once wear a varnish of this colour?

Long Evenings

A patch of sun, you were, on the bare arm,
unnoticed by the mind in reading – warmth.
I read on in memory, for what it's worth,
to feel that sash of sun, and you not far.
The sunset moves around again. I stare
upon a page shone blank, till vision swims.
And long before, you would have come to whizz
the curtains to and shadow me and stay.

I turn the chair. A blade of iris spins
in a trill of its own local little winds.
Oh, love, I would have hastened up, long since,
to let you come and sit and see it twirl
from just this point of view. No, turn
your head a little more. No, as you were.

One Off

A cool glass, the long vista to the hill,
a girl, her shadow try-squared up the wall,
mirage of water on tarmac, glinting, still.
In the mind music I cannot quite recall.
And cherry-blossom daisied on the grass.
A sun-shaft turns the pages of the book.
As once you held my eye, I watch her pass,
and someone waiting draws her with his look.

The movement, not the mover ... Oh, my love,
frivol of hesitation in the slow peal
of the skirt. (No, saffron yours, and blinding still.)
How many days that slight grace caught the life.
I could have buried all with that ... To pull
off the time of our life in unrepeatable style.

Memorial

Not this see-through stuff of memory. Rock,
that's what I need, granite. No more black lace
like winter saplings linked across the sky.
– This saffron blurring. – Something I can knock
the roughness off for years and yet still trace
your fine features; something I cannot ply
with drinks, a slim throat I cannot choke.
Your mountain-force of hair in the sun-smoke.

Above the eye-lash, single ply of cord.
Dove shadow in its curve; the arching brow –
who else saw that? strongbacked as a fish leaps.
How clear it is, and clean out of the mind's hoard.
How real ... love, is it you? Is it you now?
Let it be stone, love, where the flesh creeps.

Earth-Bound

Earth-flame, crocus under the ploughed bark,
earth-light, I have to kneel to look within.
Some peace, down here, horizon saucered, thin,
the children's noises scrambled through the park.
Half turn the head: blue sky without a mark
to move it by, though still that sense of spin.
Turn back, and let the mauving mist begin
before the sun makes everything go dark.

Earth-flame, earth-light – what kind of fool
would lay his head so close to rising fire,
so close to gnarling roots? Earth cool ... earth cool.
Low mist on the sky-line, the chain-link wire.
So cool to touch, this bloom, a breath of air
stirring the steady flame to a small flare.

Window

Your eyes, child, in the window: the steady gaze
focused on nothing special, it would seem,
unless that chestnut in the day's last sun,
as though you wouldn't really dream of it
yet liked to think the candles' inner mist
would light the coming dark. Something of her
in that, her hidden self a wistful look.
More human yours and yet you stir dead love.

Reflections cross the pane but not your face,
and mine will never touch you as they pass;
my gangling matchstick man a trace of sun,
no more to you across the grass. Yet, child,
your soft focus already blends out hers –
my love, you make the darkness personal.

Index of Titles and First Lines

A Note About The Author

Peter Dale was born in Surrey, and educated at Strode's School, Egham, and St Peter's College, Oxford. For twenty-one years he was head of the English department of Hinchley Wood School, Esher, and concurrently an editor of the poetry quarterly *Agenda*. Well-known for his Penguin verse-translation of Villon, he has recently published a terza-rima version of Dante's *Divine Comedy* and his selected poems, *Edge to Edge*, both with Anvil Press Poetry Ltd. His *Richard Wilbur in Conversation with Peter Dale* was published by Between The Lines in 2000. Revised and extended editions of his *Poems of François Villon* and his *Poems of Jules Laforgue* appeared from Anvil in 2001, and his new book of poems, *Under the Breath*, is due from them in the autumn of 2002. He currently edits a poetry column for *Oxford Today*.